# FIVE

## ON THE ROAD

## TERESA MAUGHAN

BOXTREE

First published 1999 by Boxtree
an imprint of Macmillan Publishers Ltd
25 Eccleston Place London SW1W 9NF
and Basingstoke

Associated companies throughout the world

ISBN 0 7522 1786 0

9 8 7 6 5 4 3 2 1

A CIP catalogue record for this book is available from the British Library.

Designed by Blackjacks
Printed and bound in Great Britain by Butler & Tanner Ltd, Frome and London

## PICTURE ACKNOWLEDGEMENTS

John Gladwin/All Action: 23; John Mather/All Action: 35, 42, 48, 53 (right); Simon Meaker/All Action: 28-9; Suzan Moore/All Action: 20, 44 (right), 47 (bottom); Ellis O'Brien/All Action: 10, 11; Doug Peters/All Action: 34; Justin Thomas/All Action: 41 (bottom), 58 (top); David Westing/All Action: 17 (right), 32, 41 (top), 44 (left). James McCauley/Capital Pictures: 36-7; Jez C. Self/Capital Pictures: 57 (bottom left). Peter Aitchison/Famous: 45; Fred Duval/Famous: 6-7, 8, 12, 14, 43, 57 (top left); Arjan Kleton/Famous: 40; C. Nottingham/Famous: 57 (top right); Jeff Walker/Famous: 52 (bottom). Jadranka Krsteska: 25 (top), 30 (bottom). Paul Bergen/Redferns: 13, 22, 25 (bottom), 33 (right), 49, 55; Brigitte Engl/ Redferns: 17 (left); Patrick Ford/Redferns: 52-3, 57 (bottom right); Kurt Sen/Redferns: 4, 5; Jim Sharp/ Redferns: 38-9; Nicky J. Sims/Redferns: 24; Jon Super/ Redferns: 21. Colin Bell/Retna: 1, 2-3; Lee Floyd/Retna: 15; David Wardle/Retna: 18-9; Theodore Wood/Retna: 30 (top), 54, 58-9, 60. Warren Johnson/Rex Features: 16; Ken McKay/Rex Features: 31; Camilla Morandi/Rex Features: 50-1; Brendan O'Sullivan/Rex Features: 26; Brian Rasic/Rex Features: 9, 46-7.

# contents

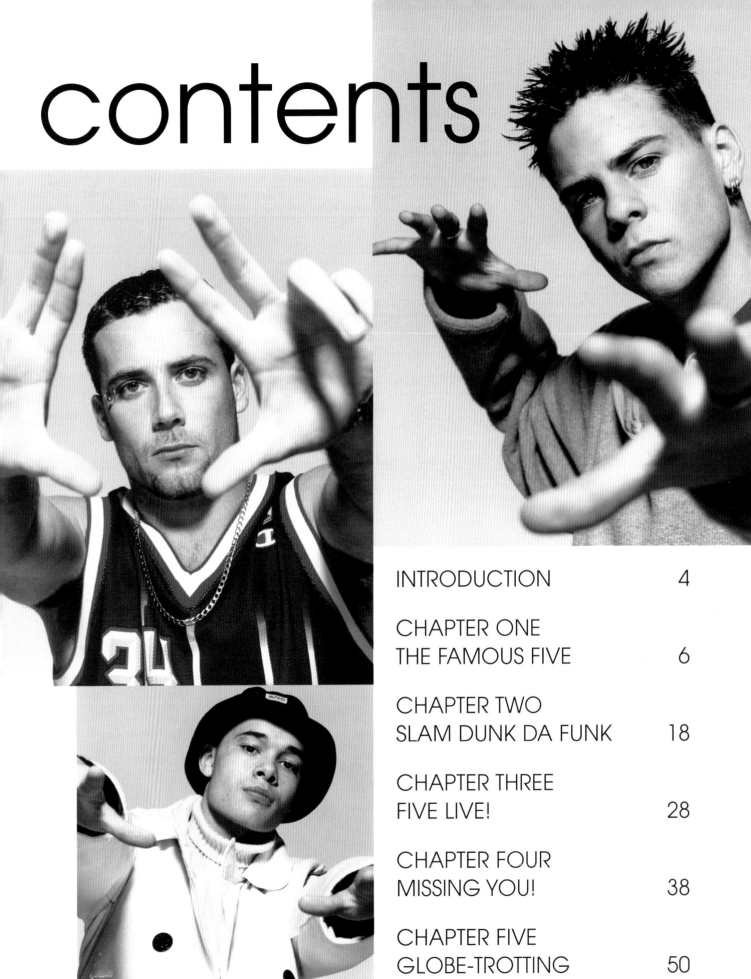

# Introduction

One minute you're flogging skimpy bikinis on a market stall in Essex, the next you're a famous popster with a string of Top 10 hits under your belt, running the gauntlet of frenzied fans determined to rip your kit off. Sounds far-fetched? For Scott, and the rest of the four lads that make up super boy band Five – it's a dream come true! Nearly two years ago all five lads, and these are definitely lads not boys – were a bunch of unknowns in dead-end jobs with only fantasies of fame and fortune to keep them sane! Now they're the biggest group on planet pop and they're gonna get even bigger too! That's a fact hundreds of thousands of fans, not to mention millions of record sales, will quickly confirm. So what's Five's secret?

Apart from being five of the most swoonsome pop geezers around, all five lads have unique qualities to bring to the stage, and we don't just mean their gorgeous looks! While most of their rivals have one or maybe two members who regularly attract the

spotlight, there's no front man in this group – because they're all front men. And their music is pretty special too. Whether it's the romantic melodies of 'When The Lights Go Out' or the hard-hittin' streetwise sound of 'Slam Dunk Da Funk,' these boys can blast out a belter of a song as individual as they are. And their dance routines ain't bad either – hip-grindin', thigh-tappin', foot-stompin' moves that leave us reeling for more! Each member has his own special following, his own special gifts to bring to the party. Whichever kinda guy turns you on – one of Five will be your perfect partner! Romantic Rich, Juicy J, Sentimental Sean, Adorable Abs and Sexy Scott are every girl's dream. So in boy band terms, they are nothing less than a supergroup.

But supergroups don't come together by accident. Five began life as a flicker of an idea glimmering away in the head of pop supremo Chris Herbert. Father and son duo Chris and Bob had already discovered Spicies – Sporty, Scary, Posh, Ginger and Baby – so they certainly knew what they were looking for! The Herberts may run a company called Safe Management, but the ad they placed in The *Stage* newspaper was intended to attract guys who considered themselves anything but safe! To be in the frame, you had to be 'a 17–20 year old male with the ability to sing and dance'. But most of all you had to have 'attitude'. The news-stands were full of magazines, from *Viz* to *Loaded*, catering for the cheeky chappie who wouldn't take no for an answer – the kind of sass and flash Take That used to show before they went all soft-centred and gooey. This would not be a boy band but a lads' band – a bunch of lager-drinking, women-ogling, football-loving, motor-mouthing lads with more talent than you could shake a stick at! It was a winning formula on paper, for sure, but could the Herberts pull it off?

They certainly did with the Spice Girls, though the feisty females upped and left to sign up with a rival team before things really took off big time. And as if to dodge the 'Spice Boys' headlines they knew would follow, as well as steer clear of Take That comparisons, the Herberts decided at the outset that four lads would be the limit. The problem would come later when five names made the short list, but that was a problem they'd enjoy solving.

Five's success would take the lucky lads globe-trotting all over the world in a once-in-a-lifetime journey of discovery, exploration and adventure that still goes on. Are you ready to go with them? Thought so! In that case, please pack your bags, check your passport and walk this way...

# CHAPTER ONE

# the FAMOUS FIVE

So who, apart from the obvious suspects, answered the ad in The *Stage*? The answer is hundreds of would-be singers who travelled to London from the length and breadth of Britain with stars very much in their eyes. Scott reckons there were '3,000 other boys' at the first of the two rehearsals he attended. If truth be told, though, he almost missed out on becoming a Fiver altogether. 'I nearly didn't turn up!' he admits. 'I'd been out late the night before and didn't feel too hot in the morning, but my dad woke me up and told me I had to go! Thanks, Dad, I owe ya!' When Sean explains the secret of his successful audition, he makes it sound so easy. 'They weren't looking for a typical boy band. You just had to be yourself, sing and dance and hope for the best.' Then again, the former winner of Young Composer of the Year had Phil Collins' approval to bring with him, but more of that later!

All five who were chosen had ambition and talent, and caught the Herberts' eye because they looked likely to mesh together and complement each other: not just solo stars, but team players. The boys' backgrounds were as different as their personalities. Take Scott Robinson – he knew he was going to be a star from the word go, even before Aussie soap star Jason Donovan borrowed his name for his character in *Neighbours*! Parents Sue and Mick scrimped and saved to send their youngest child to stage school so he could live his dream – and far from being jealous as you might expect, sisters Nicola and Hayley are our boy's biggest fans. He was born on 22 November 1979, two weeks or so after Bonfire Night – little wonder his explosive personality has lit up our lives this past couple of years!

At first, though, it was Nicola who seemed set for stage stardom. Scott just tagged along with his big sister when local theatre groups in Basildon, Essex, were holding open auditions, and he started getting picked for parts. Academically he was no high flyer, as he himself

cheerfully admits, and it wasn't until he joined the Sylvia Young Theatre School at the age of
fourteen that dyslexia (word blindness) was diagnosed. It's a problem he shares with many gifted
people, and Scott admits to feeling great relief when he found out he wasn't 'thick', after all! The
world-famous Sylvia Young establishment has recently supplied showbiz with the likes of *Big
Breakfast* babe Denise Van Outen, Baby Spice, Dani Behr and no fewer than three All Saints, so it
was no great surprise that Scott should follow in those famous footsteps. A bit part in *EastEnders*
(he played a racist thug who terrified Gita while Sanjay was away) beamed him into millions of living
rooms countrywide, while stage shows he starred in included the musical *Whistle In the Wind* and a
London staging of the much-loved fairy tale *Peter Pan*. It was all a far cry from being a five-year-
old when his mum would dress him up as a member of all-action TV good guys the *A-Team*!

Talking of imitation, though, he very nearly took a short cut to stardom when the
TV show *Stars In Their Eyes* picked him for a final audition. Though he impressed the jury,
competition was stiff and he just missed out on being televized in the role of Marti Pellow,
hunksome lead singer of Scottish chart-toppers Wet Wet Wet. Can you see the similarity?
We don't think he's got the teeth for it! Maybe one day someone will go on that show looking
just a little bit familiar: 'Tonight, Matthew, I'm going to be Scott from Five...!'

On the face of things, J had little in common with Scott except for a dislike of school
work. And as for stage school, forget it! Jason Paul Brown (as his birth certificate reads) took his
first bow in Aldershot, Hampshire, on 13 June 1976. An 'army brat', he was born to a service
family and was destined to roam the world as his father had different service postings. He reckons
he moved house a dozen times before he lost count. That said, there were certain advantages to
this gypsy lifestyle – put J in a room full of strange faces and he'll make friends instantly, while the
frequent moving around was great training for the life of a pop-star. A Gemini by birth, he led a
double life, playing at being a super-hero with his pal Glen. He was Robin to Glen's Batman – that's
when he wasn't tipping spaghetti out of his dinner bowl and being confined to his room! Mrs
Brown will confirm her son is pretty artistic – though scrawling all over his bedroom walls when he
was grounded hardly endeared him to anyone. Maybe he should have been the Joker...

J did well academically despite all the moans and groans about school and sixth-form
college. He emerged with a clutch of GCSEs but wanted more than a boring, nine-to-five office
job – it was stardom he craved, and he was prepared to make any sacrifice to achieve it. Unlike
the other members of Five, he'd set his sights on a solo career and at first had to be persuaded
that joining a group was the best move. He could write songs, and still does, so what did he need
help for? A home recording studio proved useful in putting those songs into order. With J
constantly skint, it was paid for by his long-time girlfriend, so it was doubly upsetting that they split
after Five took off; happily, they're friends now. But even though he's now hit the heights of pop-
stardom, J still rates producing his first 'demo tape' as his proudest achievement to date. His
tastes are amazingly wide-ranging: 'from Pavarotti to Iron Maiden,' he boasts. Maybe solo stardom
awaits the 'grandaddy of the group' in the future, but for now he's just happy to be a member of
the greatest boy band around.

Richard Neville, otherwise known as Rich, is another Five member who's overcome
dyslexia to get to the top. He should be used to life in groups by now – after all, he joined his first

outfit while still at school. Its name? Anal Beard! They played local pubs and clubs around the Midlands, venues which must have been pretty familiar to the lad, because along with brother David and sister Tracey he lived over a pub! It was called the Crab Mill in Bromsgrove, and was run by his mum Kim and stepfather Derek. Born on 23 August 1979, his introduction to the wonderful world of show business came early in life – to be precise, in an Easter play at his primary school. 'The whole cast dressed as chickens,' he recalls, 'and my mum's got a picture of me dressed up!' Animals, though, weren't a theme of his childhood as, due to their accommodation, a goldfish was the only pet he could have. Next step in his climb up the acting ladder was the male lead in *Romeo and Juliet* – you may have seen a certain Leonardo DiCaprio doing the same thing on the big screen recently, but did he get rave reviews in his local newspaper? We think not! One up to Rich... Hang on, he admits he recently bought the Leo film soundtrack: one-all, then!

The gel-haired lad didn't often get into trouble at school, but when he did the world knew about it! At the age of ten, he and some friends were caught climbing on the roof of his school – the police let him off 'cos he owned up straightaway and admitted he'd been involved – and about six or seven years later he was caught in a pub. His excuse was he was consoling a friend who'd just failed his driving test, but boozing at school lunch times was strictly a no-no from then on! He knew he was in trouble when his mum used his full name. 'She'd shout "Rich-ARD! Just wait till I get you home!"' His favourite kind of music was heavy, grungey rock – Pearl Jam, Nirvana, that kind of thing – and he used to cover his school books with pictures of his heroes, much to his teachers' despair. Rich was a popular lad, though those same teachers were always telling him he should try harder and realize his full potential. We bet they're all eating their words now! As for leaving Anal Beard behind, we can't wait for the reunion several years from now when Michael Aspel surprises Rich with his Big Red Book...

Next comes Richard Abidin Breen, a name to conjure with if ever there was one! He gets the exotic middle name from his father Turan, and the last one from mother Kay, who more or less brought him up alone. As for why he's known as Abs, the fact is that, with two Richards in the group, one of 'em had to give way! 'Everyone was looking nervously at each other,' he recalls of the auditions, 'but in the end I shortened my middle name so we didn't have to fight it out.' Born on 29 July 1979 in Enfield, north London, Abs can claim to be the only Londoner in Five's ranks, but his early life was hardly the high life. He lived in the middle of a council estate, and his rough,

tough, streetwise pals didn't take kindly to his abilities as a tap dancer. His excuse was that it was the nearest he could get to the style of his moonwalking idol, Michael Jackson. The scamp's messy room indicated the creative mind of a Cancerian... at least that's what he would have us believe! Abs spent his school days enjoying sport – particularly Kingball, a kind of tennis played with the hands – and listening to his Walkman during his favourite subject, art. He generally managed to keep out of trouble by the skin of his teeth, keeping his nose clean while others got into scrapes. One thing on his side was a dislike of alcohol so, while pals might have been tempted by alcopops, Abs stayed sober.

Aiming for the showbiz spotlight, Abs auditioned for the Italia Conti stage school, hoping to find a place alongside the likes of Louise Nurding and Martine 'Tiffany' McCutcheon. Unfortunately, he failed to get in first time, but determined as ever he enrolled in their Saturday school to learn the ropes. Next time he auditioned, talent – and perseverance – won out! Since then, he's taken up the guitar as a way of improving his musical skills, but as we've never seen Jacko do his thing with a guitar round his neck it's our bet this won't become part of the stage act...

Someone else who rates Michael Jackson as one of his early influences is Sean Conlon, and like Abs he grew up in tough surroundings. His council estate was in Leeds, and his escape – apart from watching Rugby League – was music. A guitar at age four was supplemented by a keyboard five years later and, armed with this, he wrote his first ever song. Writing the song coincided with his parents splitting up, so it could be that unhappiness inspired this first burst of creativity – but whatever the truth, his father encouraged him to continue and even paid for him to record some songs professionally. Like J, Sean found the solo market heaving with wannabe pop acts, so was happy to take a sidestep and join forces with four like-minded lads dreaming of stardom. Before that, though, he had one final moment of solo glory when a panel of judges that included megastar Phil Collins voted him Young Composer of the Year. School work continued for Sean until he'd completed his GCSEs, though a special tutor had to keep the 'baby' of Five (he was born on 20 May 1981 making him the youngest member) at his books at the very end. He was mighty glad to give up his paper round, though! Softly spoken northern dreamboat Sean is still very much in touch with his keyboard, which he takes everywhere with him, and no one would be a bit surprised if, in a year or two, the Five set is chock-a-block with Sean Conlon compositions. Once upon a time he'd write songs about the girls he had his eye on, but never had the bottle to tell them about it. Those days may long have gone… but the music goes on!

Five very different performers, then, chosen to form the unbeatable combination. Turning the mixture to gold was next on the agenda and manager Bob Herbert clearly saw it as a challenge. 'We wanted five different but strong personalities – not one singer and a load of dummies,' he said, adding: 'We had a huge hit with the Spice Girls and knew we could do the same with the boys.' But this was an act with plenty of rough edges – an uncut diamond to be buffed and polished until it sparkled. Everyone knew from the outset that a lot of work would be required before Five were ready to take their first bow. Choreography was to be crucial, and the job of getting the five groovin' to the same routine would be a challenge. They were put through their paces with a punishing regime most army cadets would be familiar with, the result being a ten-footed all-dancing machine that moved as if on springs. Paul Domaine was the man behind those moves and he won great acclaim when Five's first album came out. Next came the singing side – while each member of Five could more than hold a tune, the right blend of harmonies would be crucial to make the most of the material that several top teams of pop writers at various points of the globe were already busily writing for them.

Voice coaches were dispatched to keep musical matters on the right track and, by the time all the singing, rapping and choruses had been snipped and sewn together, five throats were red raw. What was certain, though, was that once they saw the inside of a professional recording studio for the first time – and that time was drawing near – the soon-to-be-famous fivesome would be awed but not overawed.

The final, vital ingredient of the recipe was image. Would the boys be suited and booted… would their haircuts be Hanson-esque or crew-cut… would their clothes be designer wear or street-smart and what about jewellery? All these questions and more had to be answered, and the lads would have to abide by the master plan. Not that they were going to be puppets or robots, more that the whole picture coming over to the public had to be classy and co-ordinated. In fact, look at the photos of the guys' original auditions and you'll find that they're all quite recognizable as the hunks we know and love today. Abs has some rather dodgy sunglasses about his person, while Scott's hair has yet to gain those trademark spikes. Though style was the key, Five would remain a group of individuals with their own distinctive personalities. It was an untried formula but, ultimately, a winning one. Success for Five, when it came, would be both swift and stunning.

From a bunch of nobodies who could happily stroll the streets unmolested, the boys found themselves at risk of life and limb should they even think about popping down the local burger joint or buying a pint of milk from the corner shop. It was a difficult transition to make, as their neighbours in deepest Surrey would certainly agree: television featured Five in a *Neighbours from Hell* series, though in all fairness to the boys they could hardly be blamed for attracting hordes of love-struck girls to their front gate. Camberley was to be Five's base — not quite London, but near enough for them to sample all the delights it had in store. Besides, with their managers' office just a couple of miles down the road in leafy Lightwater, Five knew they'd be under the Herberts' careful eye from day one. Stepping out of line was simply not an option. Given that the Spice Girls moved out of a similar arrangement in a matter of weeks, you could hardly blame the men with the plan for keeping an eye on their investment!

What the Herberts had created was, by common consent, something quite extraordinary. 'Our music is very street sound,' Abs insists. 'We're not a typical boy band — what you see is just us. We've got our own opinions and that's what makes us a lad band — not a boy band!' As for the accusation that Five are being manipulated, J will soon put you right. 'We were put together at an audition, but that's where the manufactured bit ends,' he explodes.

'We're five individual business partners who have a major say in everything we do.'

For four of the boys selected, it was a move to the bright lights of the big city. Only Abs could say he knew London and its lifestyle — throwing five complete strangers together into a new environment would be the ultimate test. Pop-stardom means an hour in the tour bus for every minute on the stage or under the studio spotlight and, if they just couldn't get along, then it was as well to find out straightaway. Any personality clashes could be ironed out before the adventure began. The first arguments came over sleeping arrangements: Sean claimed the only single bedroom, leaving Rich and J to pair up; Scott and Abs then followed suit. The boys would be forced to live in each other's pockets twenty-four hours a day, seven days a week — whether fighting for the bathroom in the morning, moaning about the lack of fresh milk at night, or rehearsing in London in-between times. It would be no bed of roses, but ultimately it would be worth it.

The lads' feelings about their different geographical backgrounds took time to settle too. 'There's a bit of a north/south divide in Five,' Scott reveals. 'J and Sean think of themselves as the hard northerners. Rich is stuck in the middle, and then there's me and Abs who're southerners. We have a little joke about it — but southerners are definitely the guv'nors!' Abs recalls the first night together in the new house. 'J, Scott and I stayed up all night, and the next day we flew out to Sweden to record our first single. It was so hectic. Also, Rich was doing his A Levels at the time and he was really stressed. I actually hated Rich when we started off. I don't know how we survived in those early days.' But things got better, six months flew by in record time and, by the time the lease on the house expired, Five were on their way to stardom — not to mention a new headquarters, whose location must remain a closely guarded secret!

Something else that was to remain undecided for a long time was the name under which they would seek stardom. 'We had sheets of different names to look at and Five was always at the top of the list, but we kept overlooking it,' recalls Abs. Then one night they went out for a meal with friends in a posse of eight. 'The waiter at the door said, "I've only got a table for five," and we thought, "Yeah, that's a good name,"' says J. Scott takes up the tale two weeks later: 'We were sitting in a Chinese restaurant and a brand-new Mercedes drew up outside — the number plate was just "FIVE". We were like, "Wow! That's it, then!" Plus our manager's hotel room at the time was number 555.' It was all quite ironic; if the Herberts had kept to their

original plan, would the boys have been 'Four'? Doesn't have quite the same ring, does it?

Girls were never encouraged to come round to Five's house because, as J explains, 'You can guarantee that when they turn up the place is gonna look like a bomb's hit it! Then you'd spend the whole evening apologizing...' Sean agrees that theirs was 'a lads' house', in which a TV and huge piles of CDs were the only entertaining features. 'We haven't even bothered to put any pictures on the walls.' Course not – far too awkward to dust! Television posed a few problems because, though Rich is an *EastEnders* fan, J claims it 'depresses the crap' out of him! He's a *Coronation Street* man. But these leisure-time squabbles diverted them less and less as time went by. It's easier to satisfy Abs, who admits he's 'a bit of a Playstation freak – if I'm not working or sleeping, I'm playing.' So if he claims the television, beware – chances are he wants to plug his computer game console into it!

The house they moved to after the *Neighbours from Hell* episode was heaven on earth for Five, Rich reveals, because it meant each member could now have their own private living space. 'It's bigger, and we've all got our own rooms so we can chill out and relax when we want to. The kitchen's nice here, too – the old kitchen had mould growing all over it!' The kitchen isn't somewhere they like to use very much, and it's no surprise to hear that there's a great Chinese takeaway handily situated just round the corner from the new house. 'I think we keep that place in business,' says Richie, 'we're in there nearly every night,' while Sean adds: 'We get about four starters and four or five main courses and share them.' So who chooses between the chow mein and the chop suey?

It's an interesting question, because Five were by now a gang... and every gang has a leader. J, the oldest member of the group, tried his best not to become the chief among Indians 'because

it would distance me from the rest of the guys.' He's been known to step forward when there are tough decisions to be made but, apart from taking responsibility on those broad shoulders at specific times, J is keen to portray Five as a group of equals. And leadership qualities the lads had deep within them were brought to the surface when Five went out on a bonding exercise in the country, followed by the cameras of the Beeb's glossy new *Top of the Pops* magazine. It was all an attempt to get press coverage of a new band by making one publication in particular feel they had an exclusive... Raft-racing, somersaulting from haystacks and charging through bull-infested fields were all on the agenda as the lads went through their all-action paces for a patient if mud-encrusted lensman. At the end of the day, everyone was happy: the mag had a story and pictures no one else could boast, the boys had bonded even more and the cows could graze unmolested!

Next would come a launch party for Five in London's ritzy Knightsbridge. The surroundings would be Harvey Nichols, the designer store immortalized by Patsy and Edina in TV's *Absolutely Fabulous*. It would prove to be one of the mega-events of the year, and given the lads' ability to spend money as if it was going out of style it was a wonder they left anything un-bought! Scott's preference for Calvin Klein boxer shorts and Jean-Paul Gaultier aftershave is pretty typical of Five's designer tastes. That said, he still pigs out on kebabs and Coco Pops (or should that be Chocco Crispies?) at any hour of the day or night! When it comes to drinks, the official Five beverage is Pepsi Cola, since they (along with Irish hitmakers the Corrs) have done a deal with the

fizzy-drink firm which is set to net them thousands. Just keep on saving those ring-pulls!

While all this high living was going on, relationships between the band members were strengthening. Against all odds, J and Sean, the oldest and youngest of the quintet, became the very best of mates – maybe something to do with their shared northern roots – while Scott, Abs and Rich, the group's so-called 'southern softies', tended to hang out together. 'Sean's like my younger brother,' J explains. 'When the group started, people always said he was copying things I did, but he just reacts the same way as me – we like the same things.' Scott, for his part, reveals that he turns to Abs for advice when he's upset. 'I can honestly say he's one of the nicest people I've ever met, if not the nicest. I can turn to him at any time and I think he's like me in lots of ways.' Aaah, bless! Scott is quick to point out that these naturally occurring groups within a band don't mean Five are suddenly going to become Three and Two. 'A lot of people are saying, "that must be because Five don't get on" but it's not that. Collectively, as a group, we always come together when it's right.' One occasion when it certainly was right was when they recorded their first single in Stockholm but that's another chapter in this success story.

# CHAPTER TWO

# Slam Dunk Da Funk

Invitations to a swanky party are always welcome... and Five were knocked out when they got an invite from the BBC to perform in one of the all-time great British pop institutions. The Radio One *Roadshow* has long been a highlight of the British summer, come rain or shine! Since the 1970s, the station's major DJs have taken the morning show out on the road, touring the market and seaside towns of the country and getting their audience well and truly in the holiday spirit. Live acts have always played a part in this, and many soon-to-be household names have given their all on the beach, car park or village green. Five scored twice over when they were invited to take part in the *Roadshow* experience. Initially, the intention was for them to warm up the crowd for the main acts to be broadcast – not unreasonable, given that they'd yet to release a single of their own – but they so impressed dance-crazed DJ Dave Pearce that they were invited back to sing for the nation live on air. (He receives a special credit in the album sleeve notes: 'Thanks for being the first believer.') That historic afternoon is why Cheltenham, a sleepy town in Gloucestershire, deserves capital letters on the Five map.

And though they've travelled the world since then, there'll always be a special place for Cheltenham in their hearts.

A lot of J's mates were in the audience for this historic moment, while Scott's ever-devoted mum was there, too. Mrs Robinson had helpfully made a banner to wave at them and show support, but unfortunately spelt J's name wrong! Maybe it was lucky this was radio and not live TV! Whatever, the exposure Five enjoyed that day alerted the music business that this was one hot unsigned act just waiting to be snapped up. And chequebooks were soon being waved at the Herberts, the kind of figures mentioned being of Premier League proportions! After much deliberation, a reported £31 million deal was eventually signed and sealed with record company RCA. Head honcho Simon Cowell faced the press to explain what they planned for these pop sensations they'd splashed out so much to sign. 'Five are not squeaky clean,' he said. 'They're streetwise, with attitude. Interest is huge. We are spending a lot of money on Five, but we know we're going to make much more back.' In the words of the Lottery voice-over, it was time to release those big-money balls! If the reaction to their first single, 'Slam Dunk Da Funk', in December 1997 was anything to go by, Five were already on the road to eclipse RCA's previous big signing, Take That. Before that, the label had been best known for top pop duo the Eurythmics, while long before Dave and Annie was David Bowie... and before him a certain rock god by the name of Elvis Presley... As they scaled the pop mountain, Five were certainly following in some very famous footsteps. The recording session for the song had involved Five travelling to the Swedish capital, Stockholm, where producers Denniz Pop, Max Martin and Jake had their Cheiron Studios base. It was a real hit factory, with Backstreet Boys and 3T among those who'd entered as relative unknowns and emerged smiling after creating the sounds that would speed them to

superstardom. The sound of Stockholm was fresh and funky... but the ingredients had to be right...

Five had come to the frozen north to work, that was for sure, and their attitude in the studio was never anything less than professional. But each night, when they returned to their hotel after a hard day's work, the irresistible opportunity was there to let their hair down in the basement nightclub at their hotel. The scenes of mad dancing, drinking and devil-may-care behaviour helped cement the fivesome into a hit machine, ready for anyone and anything. 'All for one and one for all' was their motto – and still is! Not that it gave them any extra common sense, it has to be said: on the way back from the recording sessions, J and Sean both stopped the band bus and took a dip in a 6m (20 foot) deep lake absolutely starkers! As Abs reveals, though, that wasn't nearly the end of their extravagant behaviour. 'We had a crazy moment in Sweden just before "Slam Dunk Da Funk" was due to be released. A camera crew was following us around for a day. We came across a 60m (195 foot) bungee jump and decided to show how much guts we had on film. We all did it except Rich and Sean, who chickened out.'

The press, eager as ever to find the next pop phenomenon, had their ears to a few keyholes, and in August 1997 the first articles started to appear on our boys. A Sunday tabloid, the *News Of The World*, claimed the first exclusive, running an interview under the headline 'Five hunks hitting the Spice trail', but that easy comparison was one Abs, in particular, was keen to shoot down from the outset. 'I hope we're not compared to the Spice Girls,' he growled, 'because I can't stand them!' The first shots of the band saw J and Abs in sportswear, with Rich (wrongly captioned as Richard Dobson!), Scott and Sean smarter but still casual. It was early days, and the smiles were a little on the nervous side... it would take a while for the assurance of fame to give them that final extra polish. But once

they'd reached the public domain, the name of Five started cropping up in print as the buzz got louder. It would soon be time to turn up the volume!

Having hitched an early ride on the Radio One *Roadshow* bandwagon, Five were about to take another major move in the right direction by hooking up with top-selling publication *Smash Hits*. Many bands have taken the *Hits* route to fame and fortune, because not only is the mag, with a 300,000 fortnightly sale, still the teenage style bible, but the tours it's sponsored have given many a million-selling act their first step up on the showbiz ladder. Five were to prove no different and, when they were booked to appear alongside Kavana, six-packer Peter André, teen trio 911 and 'Barbie Girl' hitmakers Aqua, they knew they were on their way at last. Happily, audiences who'd never heard of Five in their lives before were, by the end of their set, greeting them like long-lost friends. The better-known acts were welcoming and passed on loadsa tips to the new kids on the block as they travelled around together on the tour bus convoy. It really was a great experience for all the boys, and helped them believe that their breakthrough was just around the corner.

The *Smash Hits* Tour also had another important by-product – the Poll Winners' Party, held towards the end of the year at a major London venue. Unlike at the Brits, it was the ticket-buying fans who decided the destination of the awards, not the music-business fat cats – so any group who impressed on the tour could have hopes of coming in reasonably high when it came to the voting. But that hadn't been on Five's minds when they packed their backpacks and set off on the *Smash Hits* Tour bus – though it was certainly clear as time went by that their names were being called more and more often as they landed at each new venue. Prizes were all very well, but they had to be earned. First on the agenda, though, was to register a hit single... 'The *Smash Hits* Tour of 1997 was a major thing for us,' said Abs later, adding: 'It's one of the places we started out. That tour was one of the best times of our lives. J and Sean only got twelve hours of sleep during the whole thing!' Many friends were made, mobile phone numbers exchanged and reputations built in those precious autumn weeks. And, as the winter chill made itself felt, Five's dream of a hit record became reality on 13 December when 'Slam Dunk Da Funk' slammed straight into the UK charts.

No one could say the boys hadn't worked for their success, appearing on every TV programme you could name and a good few you couldn't. They were even prepared to share the spotlight with Mr Blobby on Saturday morning kids' show *Live and Kicking*, though we gather there was no love lost between our flesh and blood heroes and the irritating pink foam blob! Unfortunately, small-screen creations were to loom large in Five's lives even after they'd kicked Blobby out of their dressing room. 'Slam Dunk...' would enter the chart at Number 10 at the same time as the Teletubbies made their first appearance... sadly, ten vital places higher! Two other notable new entries that week were 'Angels', the song that would turn Robbie Williams' career around overnight after the former Take Thatter had staggered through his first year since branching out solo, and Janet Jackson's 'Together Again'. Further down, the Lightning Seeds were battling with Will Smith and Jamiroquai, so the scene was a very competitive one indeed.

Sean had been asleep when the news came through by phone from Five's record company of the single's chart entry – but not for long! Startled by the whoops and hollers of his bandmates, he awoke from his dream to find reality was, for once, even better! The only person to miss out on the excitement was Scott, who'd been out and about. And boy, would he live to regret that... His absence meant he was the subject of a big wind-up later that day as the band headed

for a promotional appearance at TV's Clothes Show Live exhibition in Birmingham. The band, travelling as usual in a customized Toyota Previa people mover with pop-star dark glass windows, pretended the song was only in the lower reaches of the Top 40. As mile after mile after mile came and went, Scott listened in vain for the familiar name to appear on Radio One's chart rundown... It was very cruel, but he got his own back when his screams of delight nearly deafened his fellow travellers as he realized Five were in the Top 10!

The song's title seemed to mystify people who weren't plugged into the world of American sport from which songwriters Denniz Pop, Max Martin, Jake and Herbie Crichlow took their inspiration. Funk is something we're all familiar with – but what about the other bit? When asked how

It was all invaluable exposure for a band with fame and fortune now firmly in their sights. As Rich would reveal, the record company were the first to spot the potential of the song as the perfect three-and-a-half minute introduction to Five. 'We didn't choose "Slam Dunk" as our first single. We were there as it was being written and put together.' But then, as Sean pipes up, 'Abs and J wrote the rap for it.' Everything Five did would be a collaborative effort, it seemed.

Five had become one of those rare groups to chart whose names consist entirely of numbers. Pop historians pulled out 14–18, 999 and 1927 as past successes – but with fellow boy band 911 doing well and recent chart entries for 702, 112 (special guests of Puff Daddy on his global smash 'I'll Be Missing You') and 4.0 (named after a computer

exactly one would 'Slam Dunk...' Sean replied that the song wasn't really about the lyrics but the whole combination of song and singers. 'You're not meant to analyze the words. It's more about the music and the vibe that it gives off.' That's just as well, then – now we could all enjoy it! To explain, 'Slam Dunk' is a basketball term which means leaping up to the hoop and slamming the ball forcefully downwards... something which means you have to be abnormally tall, as most American players seem to be. With typical honesty, Five admitted they weren't really into basketball – apart from Scott, who's mad about it – but Sean had some great news: '"Slam Dunk" has done so well for us it's going to be the theme tune for [satellite channel Sky Sport's coverage of] the NBA basketball league!'

program), it looked like digits were dangerous again. People whose trannie batteries were running down were sometimes left mystified by Five's quickfire delivery of the lyrics. But the newspapers were surely stretching a point when they reckoned dear old Abs had a problem making out the words too...

The guys were actually cookin' up a food pun. 'Slam Dunk Da Junk!' was the headline as Mr Breen revealed plans to kick his beloved fast food habit into touch with the aim of being leaner and meaner than previously. 'I want to stop eating junk food, especially crisps,' he admitted – maybe he just wanted to avoid gaining the letters FL in front of Abs! Bandmate Scott was another picky eater who needed to change his habits. 'All he ever eats is peas, beans, jacket potatoes, burgers and tomato sauce!' Abs laughed. Scoffer Scott would 'refuel' at any convenient point on his travels... and we're not talking lettuce leaves here! He recalls once ordering a hot dog, fries and a chicken burger while waiting in an airport. 'I didn't get to eat them, though, because the guy took so long to make them I had to go and catch the flight! I was gutted.'

If that was one of Scott's worst moments, then his personal highlight of 1997 just had to be the first ever performance Five did in front of 10,000 people at a pop show sponsored by Pepsi in Holland. They arrived at the gig to hear a mass of screaming girls chanting, 'FIVE, FIVE, FIVE' – which is pretty impressive considering they had yet to release their debut single! But that was soon about to change. 'Slam Dunk...' hadn't been due to appear in Europe until early 1998, but Belgium, Germany, Holland and Scandinavia would all receive the single with open arms before Santa arrived down the chimney! France, Spain and Italy came on board the ever-rolling Five bandwagon just afterwards. 'We suggested we might want to start in the New Year,' explained RCA head of international promotion Anna Broughton, 'but the response to the music in our overseas offices was so strong.' The phrase 'by public demand' has often been overused in the history of pop... but Europe was clearly ready to 'Slam Dunk...' right along with Britain! The big test, though, would be the States, where Take That had failed to make more than a passing mark during their otherwise mega-successful career.

America – home of the Osmonds, the Jackson Five and others in past years – had not been receptive to the 1990s boy band format at all. Even the home-grown Backstreet Boys had to come to Europe to find their first taste of fame. How, then, could Five hope to make their name in the land of the free with such obstacles in front of them? The answer wasn't long in coming – and amazingly it was a positive one. The big foot in the Yanks' front door had been supplied by those earlier Herbert discoveries, the Spice Girls. Their singles and album had shot to the top in record time, Geri's Union Jack dress seemingly the symbol of Cool Britannia. Suddenly, being British was hot news again – and when the boss of Arista Records, Clive Davis, heard his first Five song it was all he needed to give them the immediate thumbs-up. RCA's sister label in the States would take Five on and give them the big push they needed.

First step in the master plan was flying the boys over to the States for a record company sales conference. It was the first trip to New York, the famed Big Apple, for the lads, if only a whistle-stop one, and the response to their showcase was enthusiastic. 'Clive Davis believes there's a gap in the market for a pure pop boy band,' said a spokesperson, 'and his opinion is the timing is right for Five – as opposed to Take That, when

America was not quite ready.' A collective shout of 'Yessssss' could be heard from the depths of deepest Surrey! Surprisingly, given its basketball theme, the Stateside campaign to make Five a household name would be kicked off not by 'Slam Dunk...' but the follow-up single. And that was the task written largest on Five's busy schedule. How could they fit in another trip to Sweden? No need to lose sleep on that score: 'When The Lights Go Out' would be very much a Made In Britain production... no need for passports as the lads headed for the Steelworks Studios in Sheffield, Yorkshire, an area not a million miles from Sean's old stamping ground of Leeds.

The wealth of songwriting talent that went into crafting the next musical bullet in Five's armoury was breathtaking. Elliot Kennedy had written and produced several hits for 911, as well as 'Say You'll Be There' for the Spice Girls, while fellow writers Tim Lever and Mike Percy had track records of their own that were nearly as impressive. With this kind of pop creativity at their service, surely Five couldn't fail! As before, the musical mix was nothing less than sparky, the ingredients of melody, rap and rhythm perfect in every way. 'Slam Dunk...' had peaked at its entry position of 10 (two times you know what!), having to battle its way into a busy pre-Christmas chart – so the performance of single number two, three months into a new year, would be interesting indeed. Would Five's fan base have forgotten them, or was this to be the second chapter of a major success story? There was certainly enough competition hovering round the hit lists as Five girded their loins (oo-er!) for chart battle once more. Girls seemed to rule the roost, with Madonna, Celine Dion, LeAnn Rimes, Robyn and Cerys of Catatonia all very much on the up, while Shania Twain and Hinda Hicks were new names on the block. Add records that just wouldn't go away, like Janet Jackson's 'Together Again' and Robbie Williams' 'Angels' (both rivals to 'Slam Dunk...', and now with twenty-six weeks between them) and one thing was clear – a

good chart position was by no means a foregone conclusion.

As they awaited the release of their all-important second recording, the individual members of Five held their breath in just as much anticipation as they had done before Christmas. The dreaded one-hit wonder tag had dogged many a band, and they desperately needed to put another tack on the wall... and prove to the critics that Five meant business. 'Slam Dunk Da Funk', which found itself in a whole lot of Yuletide stockings, had done well and set them up nicely on that score. And, when 'When The Lights Go Out' was finally released in March, it smashed straight into the UK chart at an ultra-impressive Number 4. All those worries could be put behind them, Five were here to stay. Only problem was that Ms Dion's *Titanic* love theme just wouldn't move over and let them through to the top spot, giving the boys that sinking feeling!

Having invited them to their *Roadshow* not so long ago, it was no surprise that Radio One liked the song, adding it to their all-important playlist. It actually featured in their top ten most played records, suggesting that Dave Pearce wasn't the only DJ to have taken a shine to the lads. The video, which cast Abs, J, Scott, Sean and Rich as characters in their very own Megadrive-type game – something that certainly fitted in with this computer-crazy group – also helped the pop-stardom cause. 'It's like virtual reality,' explained an obviously thrilled Scott, 'with this fit girl at the controls mastering our every move!' As previously described, 'When The Lights Go Out' also kicked off Five's campaign in America, going to the radio stations for airplay on 25 March. Enthusiasm spread from coast to coast, and as the song soared up the chart it was obvious that transatlantic travel would play an ever-increasing part in the lives of Sean, J, Abs, Scott and Rich in months to come. The lights may have been going out, but huge new markets were opening up all over the world for Five and their music. It was time to go and explore them!

# CHAPTER THREE

# five
# LIVE!

It may not feature the figure five, but 1998 proved to be a golden year for Rich, Abs, Sean, J and Scott. It was to be twelve months in which they saw parts of the world they'd only previously dreamed of, rubbing shoulders with sportsmen and superstars, enjoying dangerous pursuits like motor-racing and parachuting... oh, and selling truckloads of records while they were about it! The first two singles had given them the chance to be on *Top of the Pops*, a dream come true for any young person with serious pop-star ambitions. But while such exposure was a big thrill, it also had a downside. It meant that everyone under the age of twenty had heard of them, could recognize them in the street, or could peer into their supermarket basket to find out which brand of hair gel they used. Pressure, pressure, pressure... and each Fiver had to deal with it in the best way he could. Scott, in particular, admitted that he found the fame phenomenon difficult to cope with. 'I get aggro just walking down the street,' he revealed, adding: 'People will point and say "Look at him with his spiky hair and earrings – who does he think he is?" And my sister gets hassle as well if she's walking down the street with me. People assume she's my girlfriend and start calling her names, being really horrible to her. It's so unfair.' Scott is big enough to admit that he was once guilty himself of pre-judging people on the basis of their appearance – notably fellow *Smash Hits* Tour performer Peter André, whom he assumed must be in love with himself and his physique. But when he got to know him, he found Peter was actually a regular bloke. So Scott's message to anyone taking him at face value is: 'Give me a chance to prove I'm nothing like you think.' And while you're at it, give him a little space, hey?

That request means little, of course, to the people trying to make money out of Five, and there are many of them. In particular, the constant attentions of paparazzi (freelance photographers) can be a bit tiresome. In fact, if the truth is told, the Five lads can be applauded for not giving some of the cheekier lensmen a thump when they leap out of the shadows and straight into their path. It can happen at the most inconvenient times, too, and whether Five are 'on duty' or trying to unwind in a rare private moment just doesn't seem to matter. On the other hand, like all pop-stars, Five understand that publicity is part and parcel of the job, and they do their best to ensure everyone's happy. Sometimes, despite all their goodwill, the press attention has proved too much for the lads, and Scott recalls them walking through Birmingham with their hands over their faces on one occasion to spite the intrusive photographers with their blinding flashguns and nosy lenses. Though the group's secret address has never been officially divulged, some of the more persistent fans have tracked it down. And Five realized they'd definitely hit the big time when they found one fan rifling through their bin and stealing what they'd put in there. 'We were shouting, "It's just rubbish!"' says J. 'And she said, "But it's your rubbish!"'

Another less pleasurable aspect of fame has been the pressure it's put on Five's families. Mrs Robinson found so-called Five fans were pinching her mail in case some of it was from her son – no way to pay back someone who's put up with people camping on her front garden, ringing the door bell and sticking fan mail through the letter box at all hours of the day and night! Fans of a more mature age have also started to visit Rich's mum's pub, which is a lot less bother than raiding bins or stealing mail and, hopefully, increases the takings. Strange but true... Robbie Williams' parents were publicans, too, once upon a time! Fans may have found out where their idols lived but it didn't do them much good... Five were spending very little time in their communal home. The lives of pop megastars involve constant travel, hotel rooms and personal appearances, the mobile phones at their hips their only lifeline to the world they've left behind. Abs was to say later, 'It's been a rollercoaster of a ride the last year.

It's been a great experience but it's also been very tiring! Though I've had some of the best days in my life ever, I mean travelling around the world, it's been brilliant.'

None of the five lads had any idea of the amount of travel that would be involved in promoting a single. Television and radio studios countrywide were on the itinerary, and at each port of call a ready smile and firm handshake were required. Each performance of the song had to be as perfect as possible, each dance routine precision-planned. *This Morning with Richard and Judy, Live and Kicking, The Big Breakfast...* They all gladly played host to J, Abs, Scott, Rich and Sean as the small screen broadcast Five into millions of homes.

Having moved from 10 to 4 in the singles charts with their second effort, it was time for Five to try for the top spot again in June. The third release to bear their distinctive numeric logo was the stompin' 'Got The Feelin'' which went on to reward the boys with their very first Top 3 hit. This was a very special release by anyone's reckoning, being the first single to which band members had made a writing contribution. The label credit read (deep breath) 'Stannard/Gallagher/Brown/Conlon/Breen', and it doesn't take the Brain of Britain to work out that Jason, Sean and Abs had all been involved in the creation of this new anthem. Co-writers Richard Stannard and Julian Gallagher produced the recording, and with Richard having made his name penning 'Wannabe' for the Spice Girls (along with writing partner Matt Rowe) it's no surprise to find that 'Got The Feelin'' was as catchy as a case of chickenpox and twice as infectious. This was the highlight of Five's chart career so far – but to miss out on the top spot was, Scott admits, quite a pain. 'It's really bugging us,' he shrugged before going on to explain that the song would have topped the pile had it been released at almost any other time of the year. ''Got The Feelin'' sold 132,000 copies in the first week,' he explained, 'whereas some bands go to Number 1 with just 70,000 sales. No one realizes how many records we're selling. Our records have always had big releases to contend with but I think we'll get there in the end.' The song did more, much more, than give Five their highest chart placing to date. It actually helped re-write pop history – four of the top five that week were new entries with only B*Witched's previous Number 1 'C'est La Vie' surviving at Number 4!

You could say the lads had been slam-dunked by soccer songs, because straight in at the top had come the World Cup anthem '3 Lions '98' from Skinner, Baddiel and the Lightning Seeds. Another footie chant, Fat Les's 'Vindaloo', was close behind it, while yet another

France-'98-related tune was supplied by ravers Dario G at Number 5, 'Carnaval De Paris'. As if all that wasn't enough, more new entries from Fatboy Slim and Des'ree were at positions 6 and 8! But even though Five slipped a couple of places the following week, they wouldn't be left waiting long for their first Number 1.

Sunny July was the month when their self-titled CD knocked Irish family band the Corrs off the top spot in the UK album chart. Fans had been waiting a long time for this – some more obviously than others! While recording tracks in Sweden with Denniz Pop one cold and rainy night, the lads had noticed a number of hardy females who were defying the elements and camping outside the studio. To reward such dedication, the boys kept taking hot drinks out and spent time chatting with them. The Five verdict? 'They were mad!' They weren't of course – the album was well worth getting a bit wet for. With no fewer than sixteen tracks (or so it seemed… secret track, appropriately numbered 55, appeared if you knew where to look!), it was a value-packed collection which came in some highly stylish packaging.

Tracks like 'Shake' (with its cheesy 'live' intro) and 'Partyline 555-On-Line' were real dance anthems, while 'Satisfied' and 'Cold Sweat' gave each boy his own chance to shine. Some tracks like 'It's All Over' lulled the listener into a false sense of security with a laid-back, jazzy introduction before the dance beat kicked in. Track 16, 'My Song', boasted special vocal effects similar to the ones Cher used on 'Believe', while 'Straight Up Funk' and, particularly, 'Don't You Want It' showed the Backstreet Boys the way home with a very Americanized sound, complete with raps and dynamic dance beats. So far, so very good… But maybe the biggest surprise of all was the inclusion of 'Human', a cover version of a smoochy soul ballad first recorded by electro-poppers the Human League and taken to the charts way back in 1986. The song seemed an amazing choice for the boys to make their own, but a look at the writing credits revealed its creators were Jimmy Jam and Terry Lewis, the men behind many of Janet Jackson's hits. Even so, the rap section made the song Five's own. It more than earned its place on an album with something for everyone.

Yet just as it seemed Five had the pop world at their ten funky feet, they found themselves in crisis. The pressures of fame, combined with living in each others' pockets week in, week out, had taken a heavy toll. Even J, oldest and wisest of the group, decided he'd had enough. He packed his bags and drove to his dad's, but he shoulda phoned first – 'cos he was forced to return, tail between legs,

when the 'old man' wasn't in! Things just couldn't be run away from, still less swept under the carpet. Discussions raged as to where Five were going, the price they were having to pay for fame and what each of them wanted out of the deal. As soon as the rumour mill got hold of this, all kinds of different stories started doing the rounds, including a hilarious (but inaccurate) report that the record label had summoned Five's mums for a summit meeting and told them in no uncertain terms to keep their offspring under control!

Rich has since revealed a little of his feelings in those darkest of days. 'I always thought pop-stardom would be really glamorous, but I was also aware that there was hard work involved,'

he says. 'People warned me that I'd get tired, but there are times when you get so rundown you feel like you can't cope and every little problem seems ten times worse. There have been times when I've been like, "That's it, I want out!" But I don't mean it, because there are so many brilliant things as well.' Scott described fame as being 'hard work, dedication, early mornings, the best laugh in the world, photo shoots, people screaming at you and eating at odd times.' But it's what he's lived for, and now he'd got it he wasn't going to give it up. 'I'm mega ambitious,' he explained, 'and I used to say to people, "I know I'll be famous," there was never any question in my mind. If I hadn't made it in Five I'd have tried until I was ninety-seven to be a star. I'm a loud person and a show-off!' He believed that, because their families had never seen how hard Five had to work, they didn't really understand why the individual members got so stressed. He suggested they come on tour with them for a few days, and the experiment worked. 'It's nice for

them to see why we are turning into aggro people,' Scott explained. 'You always argue with the people you love when you are stressed, and I tend to take things out on my mum... then I feel really bad. But it's brilliant when they're with you, because you've got a shoulder to cry on.' With a little help from family and friends, Five refocused themselves and rode out the storm with their ranks miraculously intact. 'The worst is over now,' explains Abs. 'When you are trying to launch yourself, you have to be out there all the time.'

Despite looking a bit wobbly at one stage, against the odds the band had emerged stronger than ever... One thing was for sure: world travelling wasn't nearly as glamorous as it was cracked up to be. Home-loving Rich, in particular, admitted that, though he'd always wanted to be famous and enjoy all the trimmings that go with it, life on the road was a lot harder and lonelier than he expected. And Five's growing army of fans had very different ways of expressing their passion for their heroes. Camping outside the studio was one thing, but the crushes at airports and stage doors were quite another. And the boys found that, in certain countries, they were taking their lives in their hands. J was very annoyed – and understandably so – when Spanish fans snatched his favourite Katherine Hamnett leather jacket off his back and tore it into several hundred pieces. The lads had been swamped by 15,000 fans who broke through a security barrier to grab what they could – human or otherwise! 'I loved that jacket,' J says, 'but it was destroyed in seconds.' He could buy another, several times over, but that's not the point. Pop-stars have feelings too, and the jacket's sentimental value can't be measured in pounds... or, come to that, pesetas.

Staying in hotels would force them to adopt assumed names to put fans off the scent. Rich got his first stalker – 'She doesn't take her eyes off me,' he said. 'It's freaky!' – while girls with the same surname as Scott would show up at reception and try to claim they were related to him. Robinson is quite a common name, and they'd simply tell people at the desk they were his cousin. He, too, got a couple of stalkers – girls who wouldn't speak to him, but just stared. Scott would rather have them come up to him and start a conversation, as it 'freaks me out when they just stand there looking.' So remember, folks – when it comes to Five it's good to talk! Not that the boys don't appreciate the dedication of their more normal fans – they most certainly do! Without their following Five would still be unknown, and when they can they show their appreciation in practical ways. When they were doing the BBC *Big Bash*, for instance, loads of female fans came down from Newcastle and the lads had to sneak hotel blankets out to keep the girls warm. In the end, Scott walked them to the arena where the *Big Bash* was being held and tried to find them somewhere to sleep. That's the soppy side of good ol' Scott... but, as he explains, there are certain times when Five's fans have got to see life from his point of view, too. 'Some people don't understand how stressful fame gets and how hard it really is,' he says. 'Sometimes you're walking down the high street and you wanna be by yourself – like, you might have had an argument with your mum or someone in your family might have passed away – but people don't see that. They just think you're being miserable. Everyone wants "just one" photo or autograph, but they don't realize that everyone else wants "just one" as well! Once in a while,' he continues wearily, 'when the millionth person asks me for an autograph, I can snap – and that person may think I'm really horrible. But what they don't realize is I've been nice to all those other people before them... but I'm at the end of my tether. I've been rude before, and I know it doesn't do me any favours, but sometimes I can't help myself.' So should you ever encounter a snappy Scott, an anxious Abs or a surly Sean, now you know why. Please forgive and forget, 'cos there'll always be a next time!

The Five's fame finally hit home when the lads returned to England after one particular foreign jaunt and found no fewer than six policemen waiting to escort them through the airport! That's one per Fiver and one to guard the suitcases! Security makes sense, though, since injury to just one member from an overenthusiastic fan could stop a tour in its tracks. On the other hand, Abs wasn't keen to hide himself away from the world, and was still travelling around on public transport as recently as early 1998. After arriving at Heathrow Airport, he simply hopped on a bus to Bethnal Green and eight or nine fans sat with him all the way, just chatting. Things may have changed a bit these days, but if people recognize him he'll still talk to them. 'It's nice. I don't want to become all pop-star-ish and be chauffeur-driven everywhere!' If only more celebs had that down-to-earth attitude...

Five's reputation had spread far and wide with the release of the album, which charted in almost every country on the musical map. The summer flew by in a blur of live appearances, promoting the singles released so far. It had been planned that the album would be plundered for another single in September – and Five were after nothing less than a chart-topper this time! Only All Saints stood in the way of their ambition when 'Everybody Get Up' smashed into the listings. The fourth track to come from 'Five', it took the guitar riff from Joan Jett's Top 5 hit

'I Love Rock'n'Roll' and gave it a funky new flavour – kind of punk meets dance, and highly distinctive. The song came from the self-same Denniz Pop team from Scandinavia which had engineered Five's chart breakthrough nearly a year earlier. Satisfyingly, it entered the chart one place above boy band rivals Boyzone, sending another hot new act, Steps, tumbling down to 6. Robbie Williams and his 'Millennium' would appear the following week, all the hype ensuring that Five would still be waiting to achieve that long-awaited top spot. But, hey – there's nothing wrong with waiting a while!

Abs had celebrated his nineteenth birthday in late June, just a few short weeks before the filming of the 'Everybody Get Up' video. The great big smile you can see on his face is thanks to the Five fans who swamped him with a huge bag of pressies! Some of those girls, waiting patiently outside the shoot for a glimpse of their heroes, were given an even bigger gift of their own when they were invited to appear in the video, set in a school exam hall. Dancers went absolutely mad, tables were thrown everywhere, fire extinguishers were going off and everyone was plastered in paint. Things got so crazy at one point, though, that the filming had to be stopped because one of the fans had fainted! Rumours that she demanded the kiss of life from each of the Fivers in turn have been discounted! If all this jollity suggested Five were enjoying life more these days, then that was entirely correct. 'It's fun!' Sean admitted of their jet-set lifestyle, before adding 'I have to learn to appreciate it more though, 'cos it's the chance of a lifetime, getting to go all over the world. When I was eleven I began searching for a record deal. Now I have one and I'm doing what I always wanted to do! What could be better than that?' Scott, too, enjoyed a moment of reflection when he arrived back at the house for a whistle-stop break. 'I was in my kitchen eating Coco Pops at midnight. I looked through to my living room, where I've got all my silver and gold discs up, then I looked back into the kitchen where there's a picture of me at school and a picture of me in Five. Everything has changed, but I don't think I've changed as a person. My life is completely different now, though.'

At the *Smash Hits* Awards 1998 the boys bagged no fewer than four prizes: Best British Band, Best Album, Best Album Cover and Best Male Haircut (for Scott). 'When you start winning those awards,' said the man with the trophy-winning topknot, 'you know that people like what you're doing.' Sean agreed whole-heartedly. 'When we won Best New Act it was like we'd really achieved something and reached a certain level. Now that we've won four more awards this year it means we've reached another level. Even if we'd only won one, it would mean a lot.' 'Winning awards is just a feeling of elation,' explained Rich. 'You just say thank you and you come off and everybody is hugging. You're on autopilot.' For Abs, 'It's a buzz, 'cos they're saying you're the best. You wanna stay there for ages and thank every person individually, but you only get about five seconds.' As far as Five were concerned, being nominated for an award meant just as much as actually winning it – especially when it was the fans who had nominated them. Awards are always accompanied by words of praise – but, like the true professionals they are, the lads love to hear what people say about them. Whether good or bad, they respect the views and opinions of others. 'Some people see us as the best thing in the world,' Abs adds, 'while others think we're the worst. But at the end of the day we're just five guys having a laugh and we're not going to let anybody stop us doing that.'

As Christmas approached, and with it the first anniversary of Five's breakthrough, fans were looking for a seasonal offering from their heroes. And they weren't disappointed when, on 28 November, the world enjoyed a new side to Five. 'Until The Time Is Through' made it the second Number 2 hit in a row for our fabulous Fivesters – though it gave Cher a shock, her long-running 'Believe' would hang on for another fortnight before dropping down the listings. Always the bridesmaids, never the bride? With a song as delicate as this, you might think Five were getting in touch with their feminine side because this wasn't the strutting, macho posing they'd delivered in the past but a sensitive ballad. It was impossible to believe it came from three of the four pens that had given birth to 'Slam Dunk Da Funk'! Certainly, featured vocalists Rich and Scott made it three minutes to remember, with the other trio backing them up in fine style. Five's time was certainly not yet through... anything but, in fact! There were plenty more galaxies to explore as they continued their voyage through the pop universe. And their fans just couldn't wait.

# CHAPTER FOUR

# missing YOU!

For Five fans everywhere it's worth remembering that pop-stars are human, just like you, and all human beings need love! And being one of the most fanciable guys on the planet is no guarantee of happiness either... Keeping in touch with people while you're constantly on the road is no easy matter. Another town, another hotel room, another empty bed – need we go on? If there's a loved one at home, they probably won't fancy a phone call at two in the morning when you're winding down after a gig, and though you may be a face on thousands of walls it's no remedy for good old-fashioned loneliness. Heart to heart communication is essential for Abs, who's still going out with Danielle, the same girl he dated at college. For Sean, though, the idea of always being available is one he hates – and, for that perfectly understandable reason, he's the only member of Five who refuses to go round on tour with a mobile phone superglued to his ear. He also doesn't like to be seen as posing.

The kind of girls Five fancy give some clue as to the guys they are. Romantic Rich, who reckons 'I can fall in love quite easily... and I can fall in lust quite easily, too!' has objects of adoration that can be described in three or four well-chosen words: gorgeous, blonde, American and film star! Cameron Diaz and Michelle Pfeiffer are his selections from the silver screen world, while Sexy Scott would go for the equally glam Alicia Silverstone. 'I think she's great. She's my baby,' he says of the *Clueless* star – that's the film, not her brainpower by the way. Juicy J and Sentimental Sean fancy model types like Kelly Le Brock and Boddingtons babe Melanie Sykes, Sean claiming 'Now I don't have time for girls I'm constantly thinking about them' – while Abs only has eyes for long-time girlfriend Danielle. It's his first serious relationship – and, as he said when asked how he dumped ex-girlfriends, 'I've never had an ex.'

Adorable Abs has great memories of his early days with Danielle, since she was on his mind every single waking moment. As he explains, 'I'd get up and think, "Aaah, I'm going to see her today!", and I'd get this really weird feeling in my chest. As the bus got nearer to college, I'd be worrying that when I saw her I'd say something really stupid. When you're in love you go home in the evening and make up imaginary situations in your head and you go all soppy and stupid. Songs start to mean things and the world's just a happier place. There are flowers everywhere and the birds are singing, even on the coldest days!' Abs and Danielle (who plays Gina in TV's *Hollyoaks*) met each other before either of them was successful. That way they know their feelings for each other are genuine; if one of Five fell for a fan he couldn't be certain if the girl was in love with him or just his image. 'I'm not into meeting girls in clubs and stuff,' says Abs, 'it's a bit false 'cos they're all dressed up and caked in make-up. I'd rather meet 'em down in the market when they're natural. It's not all about the way they look – once you find out what someone's like then looks don't matter, although looks will attract you in the first place.' So how does he know when it's real love? 'Being able to tell that person absolutely anything and wanting to be with them every second.' Not surprisingly, he happily admits, 'I'd have gone out with Danielle if she was a tramp or I was a dustbin man. I'd be happy without money – I don't need it. Work stresses me out. That's why it's nice to have a girlfriend, someone to talk to.' He has a substitute when he's on tour – a stuffed zebra toy called Zebby which she gave him. Since she'd owned it from the age of two, it was clearly a very significant gift, and Abs admits, 'It's so cute.'

In contrast with the totally besotted Breen boy, the other Fivers keep the objects of their romantic affections close to their manly chests. And why not, indeed? Back in the 1960s, pop-stars weren't even supposed to look twice at a girl let

alone go steady or even – gasp! – get married in case it put their fans off. These days, as Boyzone have surely proved with their various wives and offspring, you don't have to be 'available' to be adored. Rich has perhaps the most famous lady on his arm – seventeen-year-old songstress Billie. The pair met on the 1998 *Smash Hits* Tour, which was very appropriate since Billie's first step to fame came when selected as that magazine's advertising face before she'd even sung a note! They swopped mobile numbers, kept bumping into each other and love inevitably blossomed. It's lovely that it's happened, because it wasn't so long ago that Master Neville was claiming the band had 'completely killed my love life because I'm never in one place long enough to meet anyone.' The way Rich and Billie got together ties in very well with how he had previously described the way he gets involved with girls. Not for him the flash of lightning or the earth moving... love, it seems, just creeps up on him. 'I tend to find girlfriends when there's not an instant attraction between us at first. I'm more likely to be friends with a girl first and then gradually become closer – believe it or not I'm not that good at pulling in clubs.' He had a long-term girlfriend called Hannah before Five happened, and is clearly much happier in a steady relationship. Rich always used to say he'd get married when he was twenty-eight, but has since revised his opinions. 'It's getting younger these days. Now I think round about twenty-five, but I suppose you can't really say until you meet that person.' Maybe he could dedicate 'It's The Things You Do', a US-only single for Five that peaked at Number 53, to the girl in question. It's early days yet, and Billie is only young, but we need a showbiz wedding to follow Posh and Beckham... watch this space!

Five's very first visit to Sweden to record 'Slam Dunk Da Funk' with Denniz Pop and company was a memorable trip for all concerned – but it was also a sad time for Scott, when his long-time girlfriend phoned him to end their relationship.

'She couldn't handle me being away,' he explains, 'and she rang telling me she was dumping me. I hear she wants me back, now – too late!' Happily, rejection on the long-distance phone network didn't dampen Scott's loveable nature. And he's not afraid to show his true feelings to someone he really likes. 'I think romantic actions are better than empty gestures! And I wouldn't need to be apologizing with gifts either, I'd just be my normal, charming self who can't be bothered to have an argument. If the girls wants that then great, but if they don't then they can hop it.' Scott's secret when he wants to impress a girl is just to be himself. 'They all think, "Oh, isn't he cute," which I don't really mind! Usually it's Rich with his dazzling blue eyes – all the girls go, "Ahhh" – but recently I haven't been doing too badly myself.' That's true... because he was spotted in the spring of 1999 holding hands with a girl near a hot dog stand in his native Basildon. When quizzed about this, he went all shy and admitted that for the last year he'd been a dark horse. 'I've been saying I haven't... but yeah, I've stood holding hands with a girl I very much like, I have for a while... I just wouldn't call her my girlfriend.' So now you know! Attached, semi-detached or whatever, Scott has yet another reason for missing his home and family – he's going to become an uncle! Hayley Robinson, his twenty-three-year-old sister, is expecting her first child, and he's already bought 'big sis' a pram for the nipper! She recalls his first girlfriend was called Amy, a holiday romance that happened in Tenerife: there must have been something in the air, because Hayley made it a foursome by going out with Amy's older brother! No matter where Uncle Scott is in the world or what he's doing when the big day happens, Hayley promises he'll be among the first to know.

Getting back to the love theme, Sean lets his eyes do the talking if he wants to let a girl know he fancies her. 'I just nod my head at her and see how she reacts!' He wouldn't describe himself as romantic, but he likes to make a girl feel really, really

special. 'I'd buy her loads of little presents... One of the best places to meet girls are parties but I don't chat girls up, I just talk to them. Chat-up lines are *sooo* corny. I just let them get to know me and I get to know them, but I don't usually ask girls up to dance 'cos I feel like a fool.' It's important to him to 'be sincere, just be myself.'

J's well known within the group for going over the top when he meets someone he likes. 'I never hold back, I buy them loads of gifts and stuff like that. Everyone always asks me why. I don't know why but I've done it so many times – I spend loads of money and then it doesn't last.' His dream date is that dashing violinist, Vanessa Mae: 'She's pretty saucy,' he says of the oriental beauty. His top tip for meeting gorgeous girls is... to hang around in supermarkets! 'They're brilliant, especially on a Sunday – there are just loads of women wandering around on their own! I forget to do my shopping I'm so busy watching them. If I'm ever looking for a woman I'll go to a supermarket not a nightclub. Asda is particularly good.' Don't suppose you'll see Vanessa Mae busking outside, though! It's depressing for J not having time for a serious relationship. 'You miss daft things,' he says, 'like having someone to watch TV with and cuddle up to. My ideal setting for romance would be Switzerland or Austria and I'd get a big, warm cabin up in the mountains somewhere. We'd have some nice wine, a blazing log fire, a nice Jacuzzi and no lights, just candles.'

Whoever Five are going out with, be they redhead, brunette or blonde, the girls all have one thing in common: they don't see much of their men. Five's itinerary is gruelling to say the least, and it's not often they're home long enough to do more than give their laundry a good seeing-to. The pop-star life is a non-stop existence, and even a four-letter word like love gets relegated behind another more important one – work!

When Five are on tour – which seems to be most of the time these days – each member has his own special way of winding down after the show. J and Sean are the late-night party people, but

whatever happens you can be certain to find Abs back in his hotel room working on his ever-crucial Playstation rating! When it comes to hotel accommodation, each Fiver will 'customize' his new surroundings to meet his own requirements with ghettoblasters and the like. But no matter how late they turn in, there's always the cold, clear light of day to be faced as Bob, their tour manager, keeps them to the rigorous tour timetable. In fact, for J, Abs, Sean, Scott and Rich, the day inevitably starts not with the cockerel crowing but with the phone by their bedside ringing to make sure they're up and about. Rich, in particular, is always really grumpy first thing and simply hates being told when to wake up, but he's learned to live with it. At the end of the day, whichever way you look at things, it's a whole lot better than a boring old nine-to-five job!

Scott and Bob have had their run-ins in the past, most notably when the tour manager told Scott they'd be doing a gig he hadn't heard about... and more or less reduced him to tears! 'We'd been away in Europe all week, flew back into London and were meant to be going home. But, as we landed, Bob told us we had to go straight to Sheffield. If I was prepared I wouldn't have minded, but because I was told at the last minute I got really upset.' Poor old Bob was last seen looking desperately down his schedule to find a time when Scott could finally go home! No wonder Sean reckons being in Five is, as Jamiroquai put it... 'Virtual Insanity'! Abs, too, reacts badly to stress, and often comes out in spots and mouth ulcers if he can't get his fair share of beauty sleep. He estimates that, on tour, he's lucky to get more than four hours, which is scarcely enough for a lad to survive on. 'It's like Rich says,' he explains, 'it's a bit like being told you've got to have an operation. You stress out at first, and then you just cope.' Oo-er, sounds nasty to us! No one we know likes flying very much, and Five are no different, even though aeroplanes have become their second home of late. J recalls one particular journey when an engine

failed, and the rest of the group started to panic. As the oldest and most responsible Fiver, J took charge and started telling them to 'Just chill out!' Needless to say, all concerned landed safe and well. His philosophy is, 'If a plane goes down and you die there's nothing you can do about it, so what's the point in worrying?'

He may be a hard man when it comes to flying but J has been known to get really paranoid about the band's arrangements. 'If we're travelling I always have to triple-check with our road manager that all our hotel rooms are booked and our flights are confirmed. He gets really annoyed with me and says it's not my job, but I can't help it. Perhaps that's a bit obsessive.' Maybe... but it shows a responsibility beyond his twenty-three years that

suggests Mr Brown is in for the long haul as far as fame is concerned. He's not going to waste a single minute! But J would dearly love to enjoy the company of his family and friends more often. 'I don't get any time to see them,' he says. 'I've got a mate who I was so close to, but I've only seen him for half an hour since I've been in Five.' He'd also change the amount of sleep he gets. 'We're expected to be smiley all the time, but it's so difficult when you're working sixteen-hour days.' Coping with fans who are pushy and forward is also hard, as Rich explains. 'Sometimes they pinch my bum and I'm not into it. It's not on, you know? I'm a person too.'

At least all he has to worry about is bruises – J had rather more on his mind after playing in a friendly football match when Five touched down in Italy. It's a ritual that's grown up as Five have toured the world: they ask the local branch of their record company to buy them five sets of the national football strip, then wear the country's colours to play a scratch team picked from the ranks at their record company, BMG. 'It just adds a bit of normality to the madness,' remarks Rich. It seems as though J took all this just a little too seriously! Fancying himself as the next Peter Schmeichel or David Seaman, he launched himself flying across goal to make a match-winning save. He turned his ankle in the process, and was taken to hospital with a suspected fracture! X-rays revealed that he hadn't actually broken his ankle but had suffered a bad sprain. The men in white coats politely suggested (in English) that he should rest and, if he obeyed their instructions, would be up on his feet in no time. Happily, that's exactly what happened!

Touring Italy also gave the lads the opportunity to indulge in their favourite pastime – clothes shopping! Scott, however, already had a wardrobe full of classy gear. 'A lot of the stuff I get from the stylist, because we get to pick our own clothes [for photo sessions, etc.]. They're clothes I've always wanted but never been able to afford. I've got a very nice black Armani puffa jacket with orange inside, but you don't wear the orange side because you'd look like a fool!' Sean likes to be 'smart, but casual. I'd never wear a suit or stupid shoes – I just wear what feels comfortable,' while J, too, prefers to be informal – 'a nice pair of jeans, trainers and a nice sweat top.' Whatever their differences in style, all five were seen gazing in some very posh Italian windows indeed! And why not? Scott's still getting used to being able to afford the stylish threads that catch his eye. 'The pop-star life has been weird – now I can go into a shop and go, "I'll have one of them, and them..." and know there's money in the bank.'

It's well known that J has a thing about older women, but one 'mature' lady in Rich's life has known him for years – she just happens to be the proudest grandmother on earth! 'She's quite old and she just sits indoors and phones my mum and asks, "When's Richie on the TV next?" My mum takes her all the pictures from the magazines and she absolutely loves it. It's also brought my mum a lot of stress because she worries about me.' Both Rich's mum and his nan get regular postcards from just about everywhere as Five globe-trot round planet pop. The boys have travelled the known pop world several times over in the past couple of years, but there's one place they are aiming to succeed in above all others – the United States. America has always been pop's biggest market, and in the past British bands have stormed the country not once but twice. First came the Fab Four – John, Paul, George and Ringo, alias the Beatles, in the 1960s – and though the Yanks got their own back during the next decade, the second British invasion came in the 1980s in the form of Duran Duran and Culture Club (featuring Boy George). More recently, the Spice Girls blew America apart, so 1999 saw Five try their luck as part of this third British invasion. And personal appearances made all the difference, with their debut album re-entering the US charts at Number 27.

Thankfully, in their rush for US acceptance Five weren't going to forget their loyal fans back home, as a spokesman confirmed. 'Five owe everything to their British fans and they would never desert them to go to America.' And that's just as well – because Europe wasn't going to let their favourite Fivesome go anywhere without a struggle. 'We went to Greece, not expecting anyone to know who we were,' says an astonished Rich, 'and we were big-time famous out there. Even adults were screaming, "Five, Five!" at us everywhere.' It's been the same all over... in Argentina, the roads filled with thousands of people like a scene from *Evita* (ask your mum!), while fans followed the tour bus around in a fleet of hired taxis. In the end, the band had to take to the skies in a helicopter to escape the frenzied fans of Five! Seemed like South Americans were even more passionate in their love for Five than their cousins in the north!

But it was back home in Basildon where Scott realized he was now not only an international star but a local hero as well. Visiting a local Segaworld computer game centre with his mate Nicky Monk, he got mobbed by fans. Nicky, by the way, is one of Scott's best pals: they lived on the same street for years and used to go on bike rides and get into scrapes together. Nicky is the same age as Scott, and is important in keeping the star's feet on the ground; he's not afraid to take the mickey out of him when he feels it's needed. The biggest secret Scott ever kept from his pal was that he was in a pop group 'because he didn't want it getting out'. But, to Nicky, Scott will always be 'my mate from down the road'. While us regular folk can rely on friends like that to keep us grounded, Five often have just each other... and their fans of course! 'It's hard living away,' admits Scott, adding 'the second I get off-stage I just wanna go home.' So next time you see Five, make them feel welcome. You never know, they might stay awhile...

# CHAPTER FIVE
# GLOBE -trotting

'We've seen and done more in a year than some people do in ten!' was Abs Breen's verdict when he looked back with satisfaction on Five's globe-trotting in 1998. Certainly, the whole world wanted a piece of him – not to mention pieces of J, Sean, Scott and Rich – as they scored hit after hit in all the major music markets. With all that success and the world at their feet, the only option open to them was to give their all, stay on the move and ensure that, in a heavily populated boy band market, they remained at the head of the pack.

As the year continued, Five's passports would gather enough stamps to paper a good-sized wall as they whizzed through the airports of the world en route to making music – and friends – everywhere they went. 'We've been abroad a lot recently,' confessed Rich, 'and we're really enjoying it, even though it's hard work.' He did, however, say how much Five missed their British fans – and the feeling, we can assure him, is mutual. January set the pattern for months to come when it saw them jet off to Holland and Belgium for a round of promotions and interviews – the first of many such jaunts they'd do that year – while February brought similar flying visits to Switzerland and Ireland. At least these countries were relatively close at hand, but the chance of popping back home for a quiet cuppa was as likely as winning the Lottery.

There was now little doubt that Five's music had successfully translated into success and record sales in every country they visited. Wherever they went in the world, Five were welcomed and acclaimed as the coolest lads on the pop scene. So what was the secret of this international appeal? 'There's no big mystery – it's simply that we're just ourselves!' remarked Abs. There was talk of Spanish-language versions of their songs, but whether you spoke English or not their appeal just couldn't be denied. The March release of 'When The Lights Go Out' saw Five head off to Germany – a well-known boy band stronghold – to do loads of TV shows, while they came back to Britain in April for a tour of local radio stations to make sure we hadn't forgotten 'em. Unfortunately, this was also the month that the 'Bad Boys of Pop' myth was born, as the TV show *Neighbours from Hell* hit the small screen. It was all very much old news by now, of course, but the nation's over-thirties were predictably shocked – even if Five couldn't have cared less. In fact, they got sackfuls of mail from fans begging them to move next door to them!

*The Big Breakfast* TV show had always been staunch supporters of Five, and in May the lads got the chance to say thank you in person. Filling in as temporary hosts of the show was a whole lot of fun, and the experience was one of the highlights of the year. Trouble was, being booked for a week meant five consecutive days of early starts – no fun for the likes of Rich, who's always enjoyed his lie-ins. But then, which red-blooded male wouldn't get up early to grab a seat on the couch next to dishy Denise Van Outen?

Around the same time came a performance at the Capital Radio Extravaganza in London. So what, you might reasonably ask? Well, apart from that, they managed to fit in a charity appearance for the Make A Wish Foundation in Birmingham *and* play the Shepherd's Bush Empire – all on the very same day. That's stamina for you! June was the biggest month in an already crowded calendar. Five's first red-letter day of several came on 8 June with the release of their third single 'Got The Feelin''. Then the album made its appearance rapidly afterwards and with it came a whole rash of press attention. After a quick Eurostar trip to France, they hopped on a jumbo jet to continue their assault on the US of A. While in Memphis, the lads got to drive around in a hired car which happened to be a very flashy white limousine. 'We're in a LIMO,' yelled Scott as they checked out Graceland, palatial pile of the late, great Elvis Presley: fortunately, no one came out to complain about the noise! 'When The Lights Go Out' had reached the all-important Top 10, hanging around the US charts for an amazing three months and putting Five well and truly on the map. July saw them concentrate on Asia, where boy bands have always been big. But they had to get used to some pretty unusual customs in such exotic parts of the world, where people do things differently. And some everyday occurrences take a bit of getting used to – as Sean had discovered on a previous trip to Japan, when he was travelling by train and was given some sushi. Unimpressed to get 'a big raw fish dumped on my plate!', he gave it to a bloke from their local record company, 'and he scoffed it down like it was fish and chips...' Not something they do in Yorkshire, by all accounts!

The sunshine month of August has us all thinking of holidays, and Five were no exception as they enjoyed a few brief off-duty days. Scott headed straight for the States and Disneyworld, Sean and J – inseparable as ever – followed the sun to Lanzarote while Abs teamed up with Danielle for a relaxing time in Barbados. Rich wouldn't go anywhere without his family, so his mum and brother were at his side as he enjoyed the Asian hospitality of Thailand. He skipped the sushi, though! Soon it was time to complete the promotional video for 'Everybody Get Up', a task they had to attempt in one-hundred degree heat! The single was released on the last day of the month and simply sprinted up the charts, sparking rumours that a top Hollywood movie-maker wanted to put the boys on the big screen. The reality wasn't quite so glamorous... they had to settle for a return appearance on *The Big Breakfast*! Oh well, maybe one day.

The summer of '98 saw Five venture down under to Australia – quite an experience for them all, especially the fact that flying there takes twenty-four hours! Having only just got over the flight, they found they were booked to play in some shopping malls, where girls had been encouraged to turn up to see the latest 'pommy sensations'. Well, whoever did the encouraging deserves a medal, because the lads were greeted by fully 3,000 new fans at the Westfield Shopping Centre, their first port of call, and were absolutely bowled over by the maidens they

attracted. Shame the English cricket team couldn't score as easily! Sean was suffering a bout of jet-lag, but made a miraculous recovery when one of the assembled lovelies whipped up her T-shirt and asked him to sign her chest! But much more of a talking point back at the hotel after the show was the fact that 360 copies of the album had fairly flown out of the Mall's HMV shop as a result of the performance. Good stuff, lads!

All work and no play makes Five dull boys, so they decided to take a trip to an Aussie branch of Segaworld. Uh-oh, dumb idea! They were spotted by fans and chased out through the back gate; thankfully, the Previa had been parked just around the corner! There wasn't too much chance to do any sightseeing on this whistle-stop tour – a longer itinerary was promised for the following year – but the Sydney Harbour Bridge and the Opera House certainly looked impressive enough. J will remember the trip for smashing his watch as they sprinted for the lift. Thankfully it could be fixed, as it was of sentimental value. It was all quite exhausting stuff, and fatigue caught up with Five when they were invited round to dinner by Molly Meldrew – not, as you might think, Victor's missus from *One Foot in the Grave* but a bloke who claimed to be Australia's top TV interviewer! 'He's friends with all the stars,' enthuses Abs, who was enthralled to hear first-hand

tales of his childhood idol, Michael Jackson, who'd dropped by the Meldrew mansion on his last trip to Oz. Five were offered similar hospitality and accepted it with thanks like the polite chaps they are. Unfortunately, food and drink combined with the workload and a touch of jet-lag – left the lads quietly falling asleep one by one on the Meldrews' living-room carpet!!! Even the master interviewer got nothing out of them but zzzzz-es after that!

September saw them hit the US early in the month for some TV appearances – Abs' favourite was the *Ricki Lake Show*! – but they would soon be on their way back. There'd never been a better reason for Five to come home, as filming was due to begin for their next video release. Entitled *Five: Inside* it would find its way into thousands of Christmas stockings a few months later. The idea was to give each lad the chance to try a favourite sporting challenge… as long as they didn't mind the cameras tracking their every move. Scott chose to play his favourite sport, basketball, with the London Leopards, while daredevil J went for a scarifying parachute jump. Abs, an expert in motorsport on the Playstation, was keen to try real-life car racing, while

red-blooded Yorkshireman Sean chose Rugby League, the sport he'd followed since childhood. Rich, meanwhile, was off to Villa Park in his native Midlands to train with Premiership team Aston Villa!

Refreshed after a welcome break, the five lads began a series of promotional tours to Sweden, Italy and France before filming started on a promo for their fifth single, 'Until The Time Is Through'. By this time, though, Five had got this video business down to a fine art, and the shoot was completed in a single day. Screen idols? You'd better believe it! The autumn of 1998 saw Five on the *Smash Hits* Tour yet again – but whereas last time round they'd been the new boys, there was no doubting who the headliners were at the second time of asking. As we've already hinted, it would also see Rich and Billie 'getting it together' and, surprise surprise, it was Scott who played Cupid! He and the effervescent Ms Piper had been at stage school together, and once he'd made the introduction the two lovebirds got on like the proverbial house on fire. 'We were just mates at first,' Rich explained, 'and then it blossomed into a relationship.' Initially he was worried what Five followers might think – but, considering the poor lad hadn't had a proper girlfriend for two years, it would be the hardest hearted fan who would begrudge him someone to share his thoughts and affections with. 'I just hope people can be happy for me and her,' he confirmed, adding that the pair had 'a lot in common and loads to talk about.' Hopefully their schedules could be co-ordinated to make it less of a long-distance romance and ensure they escaped the on-again, off-again fate of Robbie and All Saint Nicole.

Milan may be one of the fashion capitals of the world – but, when Five paid it a visit in November 1998, they had another aim in mind entirely. Their date at the Filaforum Stadium on the 12th was with American beauty Jenny McCarthy, hostess of the MTV Europe Music Awards. They were extremely happy to get funky and perform 'Everybody Get Up'... and were thrilled to win the MTV Select Award, a 'Best New Act' trophy voted for by UK viewers of the satellite pop channel. The fab fivesome also found time between curtain calls to get to the local Hard Rock Cafe for an autograph session and a chunky hamburger with all the trimmings – not to mention a sneaky peep at all those designer clothes shops en route! The only downside of the Milan trip was when American supergroup REM, their neighbours backstage, complained about the noise coming through the dressing-room walls – but this was more than made up for when Rich, that well-known grunge rock fan, got to meet a long-time hero, Gavin Rossdale from Bush. Maybe they compared celebrity girlfriends... Gav's dating Gwen Stefani from 'Don't Speak' chart-toppers No Doubt!

Back in Britain, the release of 'Until The Time Is Through' was celebrated in London's Leicester Square on 14 November by two great gigs at swanky nightclub the Sound Garden, as fans milled about inside and out. *Big!* magazine dubbed the track 'a blub-worthy ballad' and its Number 2 success meant five out of five hits from the 'Five' album, all in the Top 10. You simply can't get better than that!

December saw rehearsals start for yet another series of US TV appearances that were planned for early 1999. But long before that, there were more awards to collect. On 13 December Five carried off four trophies at the *Smash Hits* Awards – and promptly dedicated them to producer pal Denniz Pop, who had recently lost his battle against cancer. They paid an emotional on-stage tribute to the man who wrote and produced their hits 'Slam Dunk...' and 'Everybody Get Up', saying, 'It would never have happened for us without him... he's up there watching us now.' With all these awards and trophies, you couldn't blame Five for thinking Christmas had come early! Talking of

the festive season, Five's celebrations this year were to be memorable indeed. Family had always meant a lot to them and, having been separated for so long during the year, they insisted they should have the chance to go for it. The Herberts agreed, giving the boys some well-earned time off between 22 December and 11 January – three whole weeks, the longest they'd ever had since they first came together at those infamous auditions! But who could say they didn't deserve it? For a band that had grown up together in the full glare of the spotlight, the chance to let their hair down with those they loved was clearly not to be missed. J explained that 'Christmas is a time for family and friends,' to which Sean revealingly added, 'If you do anything embarrassing it doesn't matter – they won't tell anyone.' A week or so out of the spotlight was clearly just what the doctor (or should that be Santa?) ordered! As New Year's Eve approached, Five couldn't help looking back and thinking about the amazing things that had happened. And when Abs was asked to sum up their achievements in the year just gone he gave his opinion straight from the heart: 'Hopefully one day we'll be remembered for what we've done. If you look at the past there were groups like the Beatles – obviously I'm not saying we'll ever be as famous as them, but it would be really nice to be remembered like they are.' The Fab Five? Maybe... just maybe!

As 1999 got under way, Five were spending more and more time in the studio putting together what would be their second album. They weren't going to be revealing its title until the autumn, but what Five fans could look forward to was a new song that couldn't be bought in the shops. It was a strange move in some ways because, after five chart singles and a Number 2 peak, the race should have been on to get a Number 1 single. Instead, like the Spice Girls before them, Five were taking part in an ad campaign for Pepsi Cola. They'd actually written the song, 'How Do Ya Feel?', with Richard Stannard and Julian Gallagher – the same team that put together 'Got The Feelin'' – in December 1998 and like its predecessor it had a real 'up' feel to it, with J the ace rapper. The single just wasn't available in the shops, and had to be purchased by a magic number of Pepsi ring-pulls. Fizzin' 'eck!

Sean had suffered a nasty introduction to the new year when a light bulb exploded in his face. He needed half a dozen stitches, but fortunately doctors said he wouldn't lose his good looks. 'I just switched on this lamp and the bulb blew up,' he explained ruefully, adding: 'There was blood and glass everywhere.' Thankfully, things got much better very quickly and, before you could say Elastoplast, Five found themselves back in the States with B*Witched – the Irish group

including Shane-from-Boyzone's sisters Keavy and Edele, who'd succeeded Five as *Smash Hits* readers' choice for Best New Act. Playing as a boy band/girl band package was a real buzz for Five, especially when they did a show at Disneyland. Even the characters with gigantic heads that wander around shaking the hands of the visitors stood back in amazement as the two groups bounced in, all smiles, ready to do their stuff. They were followed all day by a film crew and security men in case any fans got a mite too enthusiastic – and the results of this activity were seen in a Disney Channel television special screened there on several occasions in April.

Five's album shot from a lowly Number 95 to a slammin' Number 27, while 'Slam Dunk Da Funk' came in at 86. B*Witched also found themselves shooting upwards in the listings and, since the show was due to be aired another dozen times by the end of May, the prediction for the dynamic duo was even more success. And that proved to be the case: as early as April, 'Five' the album had topped half a million Stateside sales, earning it a gold disc to go with the platinum platter it had already earned back home for 300,000 plus sales. So what about the show? Opening proceedings with their current single 'Slam Dunk Da Funk', J found the backing tapes so loud that he couldn't make himself heard as he shouted instructions to the others. But he really shouldn't have been surprised: after all, this was Disneyland, where everything's bigger, louder and more garish than anywhere else! Next came the hit 'When The Lights Go Out', greeted with cheers and screams by the ecstatic fans, as the boys finally overcame their nerves and waved back to the banner-toting Yanks. Scott and Rich were up-front next to give 'Until The Time Is Through' their all, but that proved to be the lull before the storm. Three songs to go, and 'Everybody Get Up' soon had the Americans on their feet. 'Got The Feelin''? You bet! Closing the show in style was 'It's The Things You Do', the US-only single that brought yet more whoops and hollers of appreciation. Backstage the boys agreed this was one of their best shows ever – probably something to do with the fact that family and friends had flown over specially and were milling around in delighted fashion. It's little wonder Scott would get just two hours' shut-eye as he celebrated the night away. That's all very well, except that the film crew expected him to be bright-eyed and bushy-tailed for a trip round Hollywood the next day. If he wasn't, they threatened, the evidence would be broadcast for the whole world to see!

It was five sleepy-eyed lads who made their way to the Previa tour bus and headed off to the Hollywood hills, cameramen at

their shoulders. First stop was the famous Hollywood sign, which Sean complained wasn't as big as it looks on TV back home. But that's showbiz! Showbiz is also the word to describe Mann's Chinese Theatre, outside which generations of stars have made hand prints in the concrete sidewalk. Five aren't famous enough in the States for that – yet! – but were still delighted to play around with the likes of Mel Gibson's palm prints. And as the video cameras whirred, Five gathered quite a crowd of their own. Needless to say, Sean was quick to home in on the most beautiful blonde!

Lunch saw Five step back in time, almost literally, as they visited a retro burger bar called Johnny Rockets which looks as though it's come straight out of a television show like *Happy Days*. Milkshakes and cheeseburgers happily stashed under their belts, Five then decided to take in some clothes shops... and the managers of Los Angeles' poshest boutiques rubbed their hands in anticipation! Unfortunately for Five's management, they were left with the task of mopping up the monetary damage with their groaning corporate credit card as Five romped from shop to shop, indulging themselves in a little bit of what the Yanks call 'retail therapy'. T-shirts for Sean, sunglasses for Rich, a figurine for J. Abs was busy filming them with a new camcorder... where would it all end?

Scott was happy for the Five rollercoaster of fame to speed on, as long as he was allowed to get up and sing to people. 'Performing is definitely the best thing about fame,' he says. 'No matter what your mood, no matter how you're feeling, when you're performing on stage and there are loads of people watching you there's no better feeling in the world. It's brilliant. I was quite depressed one day, but once I got up on stage to perform, I had the time of my life.' Such was Five's success in the States that their proposed tour of the UK was postponed. Instead, they joined forces with equally famed US boy band N'Sync and a host of other top pop acts on an eight-week jaunt known as the Boys of Summer Tour. Rich understood the fans back home would be unhappy, but patiently explained why we'd have to wait until the year 2000 for another major tour from the lads. 'America is a very important territory, so it means we'll have to take a little bit more time.' But he assured the fans that Five would 'be spending loads of time in the UK this autumn'. If any shows were to be staged in Britain, said insiders, they would probably be as part of the *Smash Hits* Tour – a third time round for our heroes.

But soon came news that Five would be headlining two massive concerts in September 1999, one at the Manchester Apollo (on the 4th) and one at London's Brixton Academy (the 11th). The gigs, promoted in association with MTV and Cadbury's, would also feature glam girl group the Honeyz and two other unnamed 'mystery acts'. The reunion of Five and the Honeyz was eagerly awaited, since the two groups had got on famously when they first met on Dr Fox's Pepsi Chart Show in late 1998. Twenty-four special chocolate wrappers were the rumoured price of admission to this very special gig, news of which was likely to provoke some serious scoffing! But those who couldn't keep up the pace (or didn't want to risk spots!) didn't have to lose heart. It was thought one of the shows could turn out to be a pay-per-view event to follow Robbie Williams' Christmas 1998 broadcast that pioneered the idea of 'a pop concert in your living room'.

Talking of living rooms, something else on Five's agenda once their feet hit home soil was finding out exactly where they were going to live. The days of sharing a house had long since ended, and Five were finally branching out to choose places of their own. Scott and Abs had already moved back to their parents' homes, which had sparked rumours in October of Five splitting up, but in reality it was just a first step to claiming their personal lives back. You would think being together twenty-four hours a day every day on tour was quite enough for even the best of friends... but J and Sean didn't seem to agree! They cemented their friendship by buying a place to share – we can't say where, but being within easy reach of London was the first priority – while Scott planned to buy his mother and father a new house first, bless him! He'd already bought his dad a Toyota Previa just like Five's own tour bus – 'and a really flash camera for my mum, 'cos I lost hers on tour!' Abs was highly excited about the thought of buying his very first flat, having looked at a few places before he found the place that took his fancy. Nothing, though, was going to live up to the vision he had of his dream home... he'd like a place with a spiral staircase and some funky rooms, aiming to fill one with all the teddies and toys he gets from the fans! Another would be completely dedicated to computer games, with a huge TV in the middle! He was also looking forward to being able to play his music as loud as he wanted. Most of you know that he's a bit of a DJ in his spare time and there's nothing he likes more than spinning a few tunes at full blast. He bought an excellent mix of Brandy and Monica's 'The Boy Is Mine' and thinks it sounds wicked! He's got a little confession to make though. 'Y'know the video of "Until The Time Is

58

Through"? Well, I'm only pretending to DJ in it – there wasn't any sound coming out of the speakers!'

So what of Five's future? Will they go on to become the biggest boy band the world has ever known, or explode into as many dazzling solo stars as you can count on the fingers of one hand? Let's hear what they have to say about it... 'I just take each day as it comes,' says Abs. 'I don't plan it out because you never know what's gonna happen. I don't think "first I'm gonna make a film and then I'm gonna record a duet with Rich."' That's all right then! As for Mr Neville, he wants 'to quit while we're ahead, after a few hit albums, all five of us

together. All of us have got ambitions for after the band, but there's not one person who wants anything more at the moment. If I don't go on to do a solo music career then I think I'd like to go into acting. I'll never be content in life, but you've only got one chance so you've got to give it your best shot.'

J confesses his biggest fear is not achieving his goals, so he'll carry on until Five have fulfilled every bit of their potential. But he sees himself playing a bigger role in the music biz as time goes by. 'It's always been my dream to produce my own music – I used to have a mini studio set up in my bedroom and I'd always ask for more

equipment for birthdays and Christmas. I've been writing songs since I was about nine.' Sean, of course, has similar aims. So would these lads be taken more seriously if they wrote all their own songs? 'I don't think people are too bothered,' says Scott. 'I don't think people take pop that seriously – it's meant to be fun!' And that's the key. As long as being Five is still fun, you can expect the lads to carry on producing the goods.

A worldwide Number 1 chart position for that second album, being recorded in studios in Sweden and Ireland as 1999 progressed, would go a long way towards underlining Five's status as the boy (sorry, lad) band to beat allcomers. But let's leave the last word, for now at least, to Scott. 'We're gonna be remembered,' he says, 'because we are doing things and we're doing things right. But Five's not going to last for ever... I might get run over by a bus tomorrow, so Five might only last until tomorrow. You can never know what's around the corner.' Let's keep our fingers crossed the only thing Five run into when they get around that corner is even more success!